# You and Your Money

by Erik B. Johansen
illustrated by Jane O'Conor

J. WESTON
**WALCH**
PUBLISHER
Portland, Maine

To my family . . .
Venus, my wife
Poul and Ingrid, my children
Kaj and Evadne Johansen, my parents
Brianne, my sister, and her family
John and Carol Gray, my uncle and "aunt"
George and Gloria Longo, my "other parents"
Scott Richards, my brother
—for always encouraging me and sharing my pride in being an educator.
Thanks for letting me follow my heart.




ISBN 0-8251-3255-X

# Contents

# INTRODUCTION

Welcome to the Walch *Life Themes for ESL Classes* series. This is an exciting new program designed for high school and adult English language learners in beginning through early intermediate English as a Second Language classrooms. The series incorporates the most current thinking on facilitating English language acquisition with enjoyable, active, student-centered activities that are very "teacher friendly."

## Program Goals and Design

The overriding goals of the series are to

- promote English language acquisition through student-centered, communication-based activities that evolve from real-life themes;
- focus on topics and language aimed at aiding students in negotiating their way into mainstream life in the United States (and, with some adjustment, in Canada);
- develop the four communication skills of listening, speaking, reading, and writing at the early stages of English language development;
- incorporate active learning strategies, starting with simple strategies at the early stages and gradually progressing to more complex strategies, that promote students' taking responsibility for their own learning;
- promote the early development of English language literacy;
- introduce writing as a process;
- provide the instructor with clear, easy-to-implement lessons with ample support materials.

*Life Themes for ESL Classes* has a three-level, theme-based design. There are four texts at each of three levels: beginning, late beginning, and early intermediate. Each level is developed around four reoccurring themes—life, community, health, and money/personal finance. Each book contains six theme-related topics, with each level increasing in the complexity of topic content. This book, *You and Your Money*, is one of four texts at the beginning level. It deals specifically with consumer topics at a personal level and extends to include issues related to purchasing and simple banking.

## Pedagogy

*Life Themes for ESL Classes* is, as most experienced ESL teachers have become, eclectic in its approach. It embraces the Natural Approach to Language Acquisition, as espoused by Stephen Krashen and Tracey Terrell. Each lesson is designed to facilitate the students' transition from the early production stage to the speech emergence stage of language acquisition. Because the target clientele of the program are older adolescents and adults, it is assumed that their cognitive language development in their primary language is well established. Students are, therefore, asked to produce both oral and written language within a shorter time frame than the Natural Approach prescribes for younger English language learners. At the same time, through the use of Mini-Lessons, the series addresses simple grammatical issues often asked for by the adult and young-adult English language learners. At the beginning level of the series, new terms and concepts are introduced through the use of Total Physical Response (TPR) techniques (as developed by James J. Asher)—that is, through commands and modeling that provide meaning for students in forms other than in print. The series also uses visual support to introduce new terms and to encourage student interaction. Collaborative learning activities, in which students work in pairs or small groups, are also interwoven into the lesson design, again to encourage a low-anxiety environment in which students may feel free to interact. Learning strategies consistent with those of CALLA (the Cognitive Academic Language Learning Approach promoted by Anna Uhl Chamot and Michael O'Malley) are interspersed throughout most of the series in the form of Think! boxes designed to focus students on a particular learning strategy that is appropriate to each level of English language acquisition.

## Program Features

It is a classroom reality that not all ESL students arrive in September or at the beginning of a school term. It has been said that teaching ESL is akin to teaching on a bus—at each session, some get on and some get off. The overall program design is unique in that uses a spiral approach; it allows for the easy inclusion of students entering the ESL classroom at different times throughout the course of the program. While the language structures presented in the Mini-Lessons are sequential, they are revisited in a way that includes those students who are late arrivals and brings them up to speed.

Each book is designed around a theme consisting of six topics related to that theme. Since the target clientele includes students who are dealing with real-life survival situations in their social and work-related contexts, or are soon to enter those contexts, the topics have been chosen with the intent of helping the learner develop survival skills in the real world. At the same time the topics incorporate some content-related concepts that will help in the transition to other academic areas.

Topics begin with Key Words—an introduction of target vocabulary. Then a variety of activities gives students an opportunity to produce language related to the topic. Next is a practice piece, usually focusing on a grammatical issue related to the language used in the discussion of the topic. A topic concludes with a reading coupled with a related writing activity.

The student book features visual support for the activities presented in the teacher guide. It is intended as a resource for the student that can be used to support the interactive and independent activities suggested in the teacher guide.

The teacher guide includes reproducible blackline masters to be used to reinforce concepts presented in the student book. At the end of each topic there is an assessment piece that includes evaluation of listening and speaking skills, as well as reading and writing skills where appropriate.

## Practical Notes

The student book sometimes provides lines for student responses and otherwise encourages students to write in it. If for practical, policy, or pedagogical reasons you prefer that responses be written elsewhere, you should make that clear to students as you begin the program.

The teacher guide frequently suggests asking for student responses. Individual teachers may of course lead those activities in any way that meets the needs of their own students, but this common ESL approach is generally recommended: Encourage oral production first, and written production second. Have students give their answers aloud to each other in pairs or small groups and then share with the whole class. You may have them write their answers on the board, in their books, or on separate papers, whatever is most appropriate. Sticking to this approach helps students know what to expect and to build both speaking and writing skills.

## Program Implementation

This program is designed to be flexible enough to provide instruction for three traditional 18- to 20-week semesters (a typical high school year and a half) or four 12-week terms typical of an adult education program. Each topic should take from three to five days (two hours per day) to complete. As previously mentioned, the series is meant to be used at the beginning through early intermediate levels. At that point, most effective ESL programs begin to make a transition to a more literature-based approach.

The series can be started at any point within each of the three levels, depending on the students' level of English acquisition. It is recommended, however, that a class begin at each level with *You and Your Life*.

Welcome, then, to the thematic approach to ESL instruction. In using these lessons, I hope you and your students enjoy yourselves in the ESL classroom as much as my students and I have. These are strategies that I have successfully used throughout my experience as an ESL teacher. My students and colleagues have been motivated by them and have responded to them with enthusiasm.

# MONEY AND NUMBERS

## Vocabulary Input

**Materials needed:** student book, page 1; large flash cards with numbers (see lesson description)

1. Begin by counting out loud to the students from 1 to 20. Show each number with your fingers and hands. Count again, this time writing the number on the board or overhead transparency. Encourage those students who can to say the numbers with you.

2. Demonstrate the spelling of each of the numbers from 1 to 20. Have students create a list of spelled-out numbers to refer to later.

3. Continue in the same manner for numbers 20 to 30, then 30 to 40, etc., through 100.

4. Direct student attention to the illustration of the baseball team on page 1 of the student book. Have students point to, put their finger on, touch, etc., the numbers illustrated. Circulate around the room to check their comprehension.

5. Your students may have difficulty distinguishing between the teens and 30, 40, 50, etc. Make up some flash cards (they can be as simple as a piece of paper with a large number written on it) for the numbers 13, 30, 14, 40, 15, 50, 16, 60, 17, 70, etc. Begin with the first pair, 13 and 30. Show the 13 to the students and pronounce it clearly. Stress the sound "teen." Then show them the number 30. Stress the "thir." Repeat the cycle a few times until you feel they are able to distinguish between the two sounds. Mix the two up, sometime showing the 13, for example, yet saying "thirty." Have students say "yes" if you are showing them the number you pronounce or "no" if you are showing a different number. Do this "rapid fire" to get them to distinguish the difference quickly. Finally, show them the number, and ask which number it is. Listen for their pronunciation.

(*Note:* Usually, pronunciation is a skill that develops over time at a natural pace. In this case, however, pronunciation is an important factor in being able to distinguish between the two terms. Don't overtly correct any individual if he or she is struggling with the pronunciation; just continue to model the correct form. Comprehension is the issue at this point.)

# Oral Production

**Materials needed:** student book, page 2

1. Write a few dollar figures on the board or transparency. Say the amount that you write: "$1.00, $3.00, $8.00," etc. Write a few others and then ask students, "How much?" Listen to the answer; then repeat it, modeling the correct form.

2. Make sure students follow the suggestions in the Think! box at the top of page 2. Let them know that by guessing first what the conversation will be about, they will be able to understand more of what is being said. Ask them to cover the print with a piece of paper and look at the picture in part A. What are the man and woman talking about? Get them to predict the context of the dialogue.

3. Read the dialogue aloud while students are still looking at the picture and covering the text. Change voices slightly to indicate a change in speakers. Ask a few comprehension questions to clarify what is being said in the dialogue. Read the conversation a second time, this time inviting students to follow along in the text.

4. Continue with part B in the same manner. When finished, ask students to practice each of the dialogues by alternating roles with a partner.

5. Ask students to continue working in pairs to complete part C. Have them look at each picture and then take turns asking and answering questions about the price of each item illustrated. After they have had an opportunity to practice, process the activity by asking students about the prices of the items.

# How Many? How Much?

**Materials needed:** student book, page 3; Student Handouts #1 and #2; coins and bills (play money)

1. Use play money to demonstrate the different denominations of coins and bills. To help students recognize coins, point out the different sizes of each. Use an overhead projector to display several different coins on the screen (they will appear as shadows). Mix up the coins and ask students how much money is being displayed. Do this several times until they can distinguish the different coins by size. Pass out different denominations of bills and coins to several students. Ask how much money each student has. Who has more than $ X? Who has less than $ X? Use the illustrations in part A on page 3 of the student book by having students indicate each denomination of currency as you call for it: "Show me a dime. Point to the dollar bill. Touch the twenty-dollar bill."

2. Distribute copies of Student Handout #1. Ask students to identify the amount that combination of coins and bills represents. Have them work on this orally first and then write out the amount. Model the formation of the dollar sign and the decimal point that separates dollars from cents. Be aware that in some areas of the world, commas are used in the same way we use decimal points. Go over each amount with them.

3. In part B on page 3, point to the first section of the advertisement. Tell students that Jensen's Department Store is having a sale. You can buy bedroom furniture for $99.00. What do you get for that amount? How many beds? How many nightstands? (Point to each item in the ad as you say it.) Continue with the other sections of the ad.

4. Form students into groups of four. Distribute copies of Student Handout #2, one to each student. Assign a role to each student in a group. Student A in each group will be responsible for finding the answers to numbers 1–3, B for 4–6, etc. When they all have their answers, have them share them with the others in their group so all can complete their handouts. Make sure they *say* what they found, not just copy each other's papers. Process the activity by going over the answers as a whole group.

~~~~~~~~~~~~~~~~~~~~~~~~~~~~~~~~~~~~~~~~~~~~~~~

## Practice:  *How Much . . .?*

**Materials needed:** student book, page 4; Student Handout #3; classroom items (pencils, pens, books, etc.)

1. Review with students the use of the verb *to be* in the third person singular and plural, as illustrated in the Do You Remember? box. The negative and formation of questions should also be reviewed.

2. Have students form questions orally based on the illustrations in part A. When they have finished, ask them to write out each question, being careful of the word order. Ask students to share their responses with the whole class.

3. Using pencils, pens, books, and other items around the classroom, model for students the use of the demonstrative adjectives *this*, *that*, *these*, and *those*. Make it clear that the use is based on proximity to the speaker and on singular or plural. Hold one pencil in your hand and say, "This is a pencil." Point to a pencil at a distance and say, "That is a pencil." Do the same for *these* and *those*. Continue with other items in the room, close to you or at a distance. Mix them up. Point to something and ask, "This or that?"

4. Direct student attention to the Mini-Lesson in part B on page 4. Have students finish the sentences at the bottom of the page orally.

5. Distribute copies of Student Handout #3. Model for students the first item in part A, choosing the word that doesn't fit. As you model, "think aloud" the process you follow to determine which word doesn't fit ("Let's see. *Sam is . . .* that sounds all right. *My sister is . . .* That's OK. *Diana is . . .* that's all right. *We is*? No. It needs to be *We are*, doesn't it? So, I circle *we*.") Have students complete the exercises as an outside assignment.
~~~~~~~~~~~~~~~~~~~~~~~~~~~~~~~~~~~~~~~~~~~~~~~

## Read and Write

**Materials needed:** student book, page 5; a collection you may have (bring from home); a few comic books; stamps; models of trains and planes (or pictures if models not available)

1. Begin by showing students a collection of something you may have to share. It can be almost anything that will illustrate that a collection is a large quantity of something you like having. Ask your students if they have anything that they like to collect, or if they know someone who collects. Show them a few comic books, some stamps, and examples of other things considered collectibles. With your students make a list of things one might collect. Almost anything goes. Use a sense of humor to get the ball rolling. Post the list in the room for future reference.

2. Direct student attention to the Think! box on page 5. Point out that reading the questions in advance will help them read for specific information. They will be more focused on the reading. Go over the questions with them.

3. Read the first paragraph with students. Have them answer any of the questions that they can. Ask students to read the second paragraph silently and answer any questions related to it. Have them continue in the same manner with the rest of the reading.

4. Have students write out the answers to the questions in part B. Go over the answers with them when they finish.

5. Suggest to your students that they write about collections they have, or that someone they know has. Be sure to encourage them to list their ideas prior to starting to write.

## Check Your Understanding

**Materials needed:** Student Handout #4

1. The assessment for this unit is in two parts. You will administer the first part individually. It consists of questions that the students answer orally. You will ask each student up to five of the following questions (or create your own) and rate each response +, O, or –. A "+" indicates very good mastery of the terms, an "O" is satisfactory/good, and a "–" indicates more practice is needed. Rate responses on students handouts; then let them continue the test. An acceptable level for continuing on to the next unit would be three out of five correct responses. If students don't attain the desired level of competence, allow them time to practice and try again.

(1) (Have some coins in front of the student.) Show me a penny (nickel, dime, quarter, half-dollar, etc.).

(2) (Place a quantity of money in front of the student.) How much is this?

(3) (Write a number for the student.) What number is this?

(4) (Show the student an ad with a price from the newspaper.) How much is that?

(5) Are you going to school on Saturday?

(6) (Write down a money amount.) How much is this?

(7) What are you going to do tomorrow?

(8) What are you going to do tonight?

2. As the second part of the assessment, students finish the rest of the handout on their own. Complete sentences and perfect grammar are not the objective, nor is punctuation an issue at this point. Look for the ability to communicate ideas.

---

## Answer Key

### Student Handout #1—Coins and Bills (page 6)

| | |
|---|---|
| 1. $1.58 | 5. $66.81 |
| 2. $9.07 | 6. $36.85 |
| 3. $16.99 | 7. $67.56 |
| 4. $47.63 | |

### Student Handout #2—How Many Are There? (page 7)

Answers will vary depending on the makeup of the classroom, school, and community.

### Student Handout #3— *This, That, These,* and *Those* (page 8)

A. 1. c

  2. b

  3. d

  4. c

  5. a

B. 1. That is (That's) a bicycle.

  2. These are pencils.

  3. Those are apples.

  4. That is a soccer ball.

  5. This is a watch.

  6. Those are girls (women).

### Student Handout #4—Check Your Understanding (page 9)

A. See the teacher guide for this section.

B. 1. Those are (some) pencils.

  2. This is a book.

  3. These are (some) oranges.

  4. That is a baseball.

C. Answers will vary. Focus on student's ability to communicate ideas effectively. Correct only the targeted grammar in this section.

# 1. Coins and Bills

**How much money is there?**

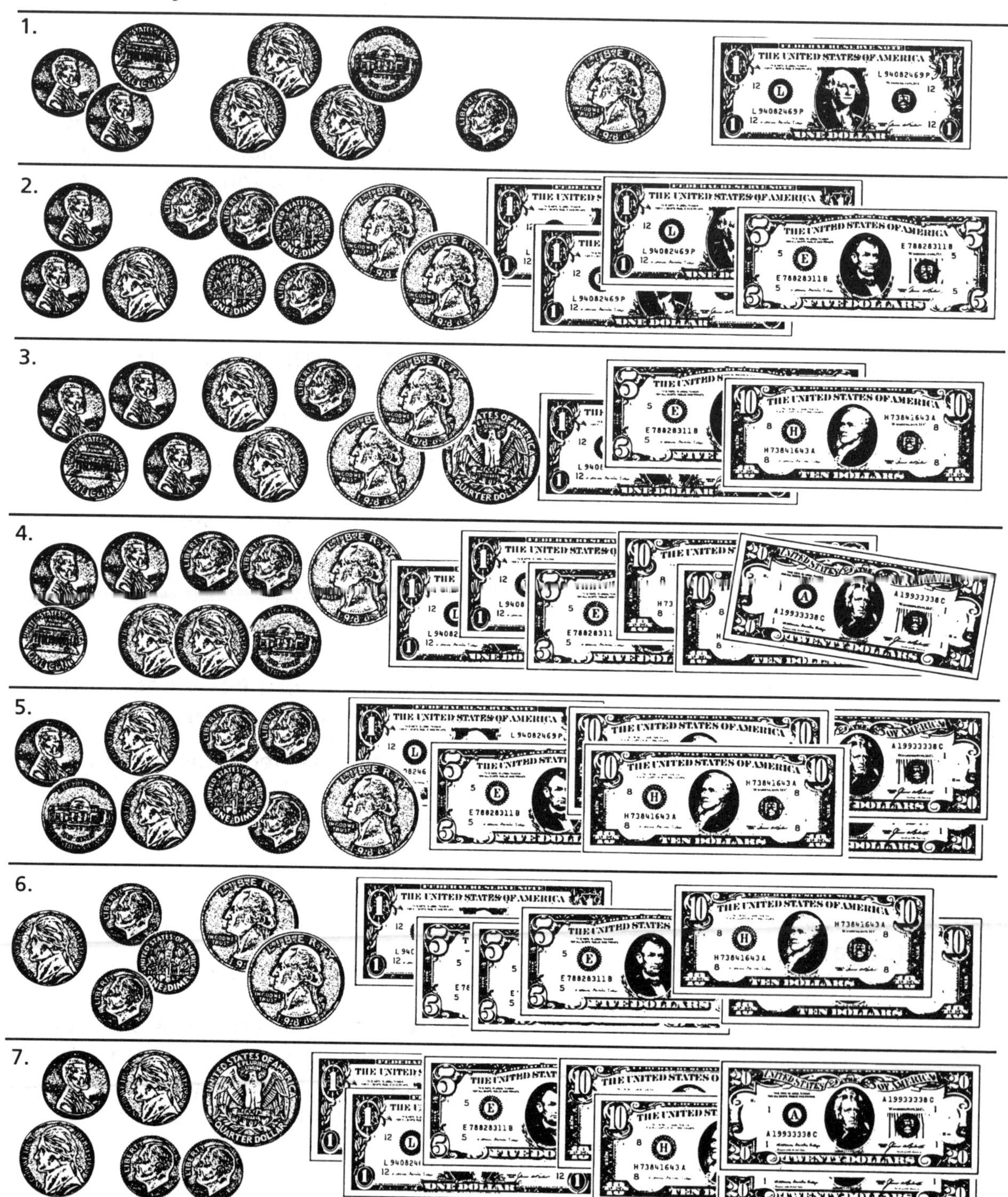

# 2. How Many Are There?

1. How many desks and tables are there in the classroom?

   _______________________________________________________________

2. How many English books are there in the classroom?

   _______________________________________________________________

3. How many pages are there in your English book?

   _______________________________________________________________

4. How many men are there in the class?

   _______________________________________________________________

5. How many women are there in the class?

   _______________________________________________________________

6. How many students are there in your school? (Ask your teacher.)

   _______________________________________________________________

7. How many supermarkets are there in your community?

   _______________________________________________________________

8. How many maps are there on the walls of this room?

   _______________________________________________________________

9. How many libraries are there in this neighborhood?

   _______________________________________________________________

10. How many teachers are there at your school? (Ask your teacher.)

    _______________________________________________________________

11. How many movie theaters are there in your neighborhood?

    _______________________________________________________________

12. How many buttons are there in your group? (Ask your teacher what a button is.)

    _______________________________________________________________

# 3. *This*, *That*, *These*, and *Those*

**A. Draw a circle around the word that doesn't belong:**

|   1. is   |   2. aren't   |   3. is   |   4. are   |   5. isn't   |
|---|---|---|---|---|
| (a) Sam | (a) Bill and I | (a) Mike | (a) You and I | (a) I |
| (b) my sister | (b) I | (b) my car | (b) our sisters | (b) she |
| (c) we | (c) They | (c) the cat | (c) my mother | (c) Henry |
| (d) Diana | (d) You | (d) You | (d) They | (d) the school |

**B. Look at the picture. Then write a sentence using *this*, *that*, *these*, or *those*:**

1. _______________________________________________

2. _______________________________________________

3. _______________________________________________

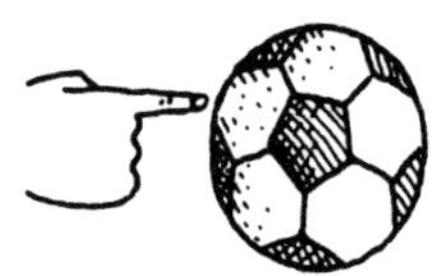

4. _______________________________________________

5. _______________________________________________

6. _______________________________________________

# 4. Check Your Understanding

**A. Answer the questions the teacher asks you.**

+ = very good   **O** = good   – = need more practice

1. _________   2. _________   3. _________   4. _________   5. _________

**B. Look at the picture. Write a sentence using *this*, *that*, *these*, or *those*:**

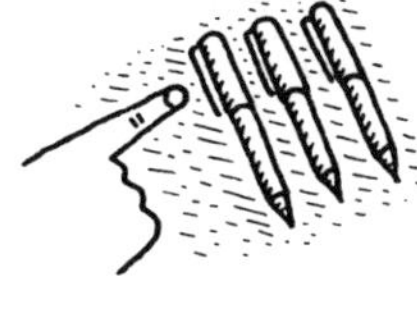

1. _______________________________________________________

2. _______________________________________________________

3. _______________________________________________________

4. _______________________________________________________

**C. Describe a collection that you know about** (Is it your collection or a friend's? How many things are in the collection? How much do they cost?):

_______________________________________________________

_______________________________________________________

_______________________________________________________

_______________________________________________________

_______________________________________________________

   **9**   *Life Themes for ESL Classes: You and Your Money – 1*

# MEASUREMENTS



**Materials needed:** student book, page 6; measuring implements (ruler, yardstick, measuring cup, scale, pint container, quart container, gallon container); Student Handout #5

1. Display the measuring implements on a table or counter so that all can see. Begin by showing students an inch on the ruler. Measure a few things, announcing the measurement as you do so: "My pencil is 8 inches long. His paper is $8\frac{1}{2}$ inches wide." Do the same for other units of measurement (use water for liquid measurements).

2. Use TPR (Total Physical Response) to pass the implements around ("Take the cup." "Give the cup to her." "Put the gallon on the floor." "Stand next to the quart."). Demonstrate the differences between height, weight, length, and width. Illustrate those terms on the board or overhead (include the notion that mountains are high; people, trees, and buildings are tall).

3. Direct student attention to the illustrations on page 6 of the student book. Have students point to, touch, or otherwise indicate the unit of measurement as you say it (be sure to mix up the order).

4. Show students an item such as a book. Ask them how you measure its weight. Is it weighed in ounces? (It can be.) Is it weighed in pounds? (If it is a large book, yes.) Is it weighed in tons? (It is probably not.) What about its width? inches, feet, yards, miles? Do this with several items around the room, demonstrating the use of the different units of measurement.

5. Distribute copies of Student Handout #5, which you may wish to assign as homework. Have students identify at least three items that are measured as indicated in the columns. Go over student responses by creating a class chart or by listing their responses on an overhead transparency.

## Oral Production

**Materials needed:** student book, page 7; Student Handout #6; 1-meter ruler (borrow one from a science teacher); ruler and yardstick; a bathroom scale

1. Begin by asking students how long a meter is. Is it longer or shorter than an inch? a foot? a yard? Ask students how tall they are in their country. Do they measure themselves in meters, or in feet and inches? Do they weigh themselves

in pounds or kilos? Use the measuring sticks to compare the difference between standard measurements used in this country and metric measurements used in other parts of the world.

2. Ask students to look at the picture in part A on page 7 of the student book. What are the people measuring? Who is taller? Are the people the same height?

3. Read to the students the dialogue in part A, changing voices to indicate a change in speakers. Ask a few comprehension questions to check for understanding. Ask a few volunteers to read a part for the class.

4. With the yardstick or a tape measure, measure the height of everyone in class, using feet and inches. Share with students the idea that there are 12 inches in a foot and 3 feet in a yard. We use inches and feet when we measure how tall people are (not yards, which are used for length and distance). Make sure that all the students know their height in feet and inches.

5. Have students look at the different dimensions in the box in part B. Following the pattern in the questions, have students compare metric and standard measurements. Make sure that they understand that in this country, we use standard measurements (inches, feet,

ounces, etc.). Have students answer the questions with a partner. Then ask each pair to create a few of their own questions concerning comparisons between standard and metric measurements. Have them give their questions to another pair to answer. (*Note:* The dialogue in part C will be used as an introduction to the practice on page 9 of the student book.)

6. Distribute copies of Student Handout #6, one per student. This can be assigned as an outside activity if you are sure that students have access to the tools needed to complete it. Explain that a scavenger hunt is a game in which players try to find information or objects on a list. In this hunt, students will weigh and measure to "find" items asked for in the activity. Make available to them the tools needed to make the different measurements: bathroom scale, yardsticks and rulers, measuring tapes (if available), etc. Give them about 20 minutes (more if the class is large) to complete the activity. If you have any recent arrivals, pair them up with more experienced students. Monitor the class constantly during the activity. Roam the classroom, asking clarifying questions to check understanding. Process the activity by asking students to share their results with the class.

## Measure Your World

**Materials needed:** student book, page 8; measuring tools as in the preceding activity; colored pencils or pens; items to measure as listed on page 8 (a box of magazines, notebook paper, etc.)

1. Direct students' attention to page 8. Divide the class into groups of four. Give each student in each group a different colored pencil or pen so that there are four different colors in each group. On a separate sheet of paper (or on one

student's book page, students will take turns recording the group's answers to the questions. The answers should be written in four colors in four distinct handwritings. Each student will be responsible for recording three of the group's answers.

2. Before students begin, have them look at the questions. Is there anything they don't understand? Help to clarify any of those concerns. Model for them height, width, length, and weight.

3. Allow about 30 minutes for the groups to finish the activity. Circulate to be sure that they are sharing responsibilities. Don't allow one student to dominate, and make sure they understand that they may not share pencils; everyone contributes.

4. Process the activity by asking groups to share their findings with the whole class. Do the measurements for them to check for correctness.

## Practice: *Some* and *Any*

**Materials needed:** student book, pages 7 (part C) and 9

1. Direct student attention back to page 7, part C. Ask, "What word do we use if we don't know how much we have of something?" Write the word *some* on the board. How much is that? How much is *some*? "Can you tell me how many waters there are in a glass of water?" If we can't answer the question "How many?" then we use the word *some*, as in "There's some water in the glass."

2. Use the dialogue in part C to illustrate the point. Read it to the students; then ask a few questions to check their understanding. How much coffee is in the pot? Can we ask "How many?" It is an "uncountable." We can't count coffee, or any liquid for that matter, so *is some* is most often used. How many apples are in the refrigerator? We don't know for sure, but we *can* count them, so we use the plural form, *are some*. Continue by demonstrating the use of *any* to form questions, as in "Do you want any mustard?" and in the negative, "I don't want any mustard."

3. Read the dialogue again. Then have students practice it in pairs, changing roles at least once.

4. Direct student attention to the Mini-Lesson at the top of page 9. Use these and other examples to demonstrate the formation of affirmatives, negatives, and questions using *some* and *any*.

5. Have students, in pairs, use the illustrations in part A to create statements using *some*. Have them do the exercise orally first and then in writing. Ask students to follow the same procedure as they do parts B and C.

## Read and Write

**Materials needed:** student book, page 10; Student Handout #7

1. Using what they now know about the differences in measuring between here and their home country, have students make "What I know" statements to each other in pairs or triads. Have them describe to each other what they now understand about the differences in measuring between the two systems. They might make a list of the things they now understand to be different. Ask pairs or triads to share what they listed with the whole class.

2. Begin the reading by having students look at the pictures. What measurements are illustrated? How are they different from measurements in their home country? Read the first paragraph for them. Check for comprehension.

3. Ask a volunteer to read the second paragraph. Again, check for comprehension. See if anyone in class can calculate how many kilometers per hour 100 miles per hour is. (161 kph) How many miles per hour is 100 kph? (62 mph)

4. Ask students to read the rest of the piece silently. When all have finished, check for comprehension.

5. Ask students if they have found any other differences between life here and life in their home country. On poster paper or an overhead transparency, list some of their responses, using a T-chart as on Student Handout #7. Model for them how to compare the two countries, using measurements as a starting point.

6. Distribute copies of Student Handout #7. Ask students to respond to the writing prompt by listing some of the other differences they have found, as in the examples provided. Then have them use their chart to begin writing about those differences they have identified.

## Check Your Understanding

**Materials needed:** Student Handout #8

1. The assessment for this unit is in two parts. You will administer the first part individually. It consists of questions that the students answer orally. You will ask each student up to five of the following questions (or create your own) and rate each response +, O, or –. A "+" indicates very good mastery of the terms, an "O" is satisfactory/good, and a "–" indicates more practice is needed. Rate student responses on the handouts; then let the students continue the test. An acceptable level for continuing on to the next unit would be three out of five correct responses. If students don't attain the desired level of competence, allow them time to practice and try again.

(1) (Show student a yardstick.) Show me an inch (5 inches, 2 feet, a yard).

(2) How many inches are in a foot?

(3) How many feet are in a yard?

(4) (Place a cup, pint, quart, and gallon on the table and point to one.) How much is that?

(5) How tall are you?

(6) (Show a picture from page 9 of the student book.) What is there?

(7) (Show the student an empty glass or cup.) Is there any water (coffee) in the glass (cup)?

(8) What's longer, a mile or a kilometer (inch or centimeter, yard or meter)?

2. Allow students to finish the rest of the assessment on their own. Complete sentences and perfect grammar are not the objective, nor is punctuation an issue at this point. Look for the ability to communicate ideas.

---

## Answer Key

### Student Handout #5—Units of Measurement (page 16)

*Possible answers:*

**How Tall?**

Inches:  a table, a desk, a lamp, an animal

Feet:  a person, a table, a bookcase, a door, a wall map, a window, a tree, a building

**How Long?**

Inches:  a pencil, a pen, a ruler, a yardstick, a piece of paper, a book, a notebook

Feet:  a yardstick, a room, a hallway, a building, a board

Yards:  a football field, a soccer field, a street, a yard (larger items)

Miles:  a highway, a trip, a beach, a race

**How Wide?**

Inches:  a book, a piece of paper, a door, a window

Feet:  a room, a building, a large tree, a hallway

Yards:  a football field, a soccer field, a street, a yard (larger items)

Miles:  a beach, a planet, a star (very large)

**How High?**

Inches:  a jump, water level, a mark on the wall

Feet:  a mountain, snow, an airplane in the air, a building

Miles:  an airplane in the air, planets, stars, satellites, rockets (things in the sky)

**What Does It Weigh?**

Ounces:  a pencil/pen, liquid, small amounts of food, a letter, a baby

Pounds:  a package (box), a person, an animal, large amounts of food

Tons:  an elephant, a car, a truckload, a train load (very large amounts)

## How Much Is There?

Cups:  flour, sugar, milk (other liquids of small quantity)

Pints:  cream, liquor, small carton of milk

Quart:  milk, liquor, soda, juice, ice cream, oil for your car

Gallon:  gas, milk, ice cream, fruit drink, water

## Student Handout #6—Scavenger Hunt (page 17)

Answers will vary.

## Student Handout #7—Making Comparisons (page 18)

This is to be used as the first step in the writing process. Check to make sure that the comparisons students are making are valid.

## Student Handout #8—Check Your Understanding (page 19)

A.  See the teacher guide for this section.

B. 1.  There isn't any coffee (in the cup).

2.  There are some apples (in the refrigerator).

3.  There is (There's) some water (in the glass).

4.  There aren't any oranges (in the box).

C.  Answers will vary. Check student writings for accuracy of comparisons. Focus on effective communication of ideas and use of the target vocabulary.

Name _______________________________________________  Date _______________________________________

# 5.  Units of Measurement

**Name three or more items that you measure like this:**

| How Tall? | How Long? | How Wide? |
|---|---|---|
| Inches:<br><br>*a table*<br><br><br><br><br><br>Feet: | Inches:<br><br>*a pencil*<br><br><br>Feet:<br><br><br>Yards:<br><br><br>Miles: | Inches:<br><br><br><br>Feet:<br><br><br>Yards:<br><br><br>Miles: |

| How High? | What Does It Weigh? | How Much Is There? |
|---|---|---|
| Inches:<br><br>Feet:<br><br>Yards:<br><br>Miles: | Ounces:<br><br>Pounds:<br><br>Tons: | Cup:<br><br>Pint:<br><br>Quart:<br><br>Gallon: |

# 6. Scavenger Hunt

**To win this scavenger hunt, you must do all eight problems. If you get all eight, you win!**

1. Find something that weighs more than 3 pounds, but less than 10 pounds

   What is it? _______________________________________________

2. Find something that is taller than 6 inches but shorter than 3 feet.

   What is it? _______________________________________________

3. What is the height of four people in your English class? (Ask them, "How tall are you?")

   _______________________________________________

4. Find something that weighs more than 10 pounds but less than 30 pounds.

   What is it? _______________________________________________

5. How long are your arms? (Measure both arms.)

   _______________________________________________

6. How many inches long are both of your feet (one foot + other foot)?

   _______________________________________________

7. Find something that weighs less than 100 pounds but more than 30 pounds.

   What is it? _______________________________________________

8. Find something that weighs less than 1 pound.

   What is it? _______________________________________________

   17   *Life Themes for ESL Classes: You and Your Money – 1*

# 7. Making Comparisons

**Use this T-chart to compare life here and life in your country:**

| Life in This Country | Life in My Country |
|---|---|
| *We measure in inches, feet, yards, and miles.* | *We measure in centimeters, meters, and kilometers.* |

# 8. Check Your Understanding

**A. Answer the questions the teacher asks you.**

**+** = very good   **O** = good   **–** = need more practice

1. _________   2. _________   3. _________   4. _________   5. _________

**B. Look at the picture. Write a sentence using *some* or *any*:**

1. _______________________________________________

2. _______________________________________________

3. _______________________________________________

4. _______________________________________________

**C. Describe how life here is different from that in your home country** (Do people measure differently? Is the food different? Is the money different?):

_______________________________________________

_______________________________________________

_______________________________________________

_______________________________________________

_______________________________________________

# BUYING

## Vocabulary Input

**Materials needed:** student book, page 11; newspaper ads for different products sold in varying quantities; overhead transparency of student book, page 11; Student Handout #9

1. Show students ads from local newspapers that promote familiar products (e.g., food, shoes) sold in different quantities as identified in the Key Words box on page 11. Discuss some of the examples with them. How are fruits sold? (some by the pound, others $X$ for $1.00, etc.) How are shoes sold? (a pair)

2. Using a transparency of page 11, point out to students each of the various examples of multiples in buying. Use TPR techniques ("point to," "touch," "show me," etc.) to check for understanding. Ask questions of those who are more experienced: "What sells by the dozen?" "What sells in pairs?" "What can you buy at two for $X$ amount of dollars?"

3. Have students, in pairs, begin to ask each other questions about the units used in selling. If the group you are working with is of mixed abilities, pair a more experienced student with a beginning student. Have the experienced student ask questions of the beginner.

4. Distribute copies of Student Handout #9. Have students look at newspaper ads, catalogs, magazines, or any other resource available to them to find and list items that are sold in the multiples indicated on the chart. This can be assigned as an outside activity if students have access to the resources above. If you assign the handout as a classroom activity, have students form pairs or triads to work collaboratively. Process the activity by having students share their results with the whole class. Students should notice that there are more items sold in certain multiples. They will not find as many items sold in threes, for example, as by the dozen.

## Oral Production

**Materials needed:** poster paper and marking pen; student book, page 12; Student Handout #10

1. On poster paper, model writing a shopping list for your students. Say, "I need some new shoes (point to your shoes)." Write shoes on your list. Model a few more items, and then ask some of your students what they need. Add their responses to your list. Also add a few more items, saying, "I don't need ______, but I want one (add to list)." "I don't

need _____ , but I want one (add to list)." Post the shopping list.

2. Continue by explaining to students that they are going to listen to a conversation. Have them first look at the picture in part A on page 12, while they cover the text with a piece of paper. What are the people talking about? Does someone need something? What does she need? Where can she buy them?

3. While they are still covering the text and looking at the picture, read to students the first dialogue, varying your voice to indicate a change in speakers. Ask a few comprehension check questions. Read the conversation again, this time with students following in the text. Ask a few volunteers to read the two parts for the class.

4. Continue with the dialogue in part B. Have students cover the text, predict the content of the conversation based on what they see in the picture, listen to you read while they cover the text, then read silently while you read again.

5. Have students form pairs to practice the two dialogues together. Make sure each partner has the opportunity to practice both roles.

6. Ask students, in their pairs, to practice stating the needs illustrated in part C.

7. Distribute copies of Student Handout #10. Ask students to identify at least 10 things they really *need* in one column, and 10 things they don't really need, but that they *want* in the other. If they don't know the word for an item, have them draw a picture. Have them share their responses. Help them name those items they drew. Write their responses on a sheet of poster paper and display it in the classroom. Compare this list with the shopping list you created at the beginning of the dialogues.

## Which Is the Better Buy?

**Materials needed:** student book, page 13; variety of cans of fruit and vegetables of different sizes; supermarket ads from local newspapers and magazines; cut-and-paste tools

1. If possible, bring into class canned goods of different sizes and show them to students. Point out the weight indicated on the label. "How many ounces are in this can?" Write the size on the board or overhead transparency. Show them another size (of the same product, if possible). Give each size a price. Ask them which one is a better price—two of the small can at one price, or one large can at the other price. Show them that *usually* the larger the package, the better the price is per ounce. Illustrate using simple math to show the price per ounce.

2. Use part A on page 13 of the student book to reinforce unit pricing. Have students look at box #1. Two six-packs of soda are $2.75 each (12 sodas for $5.50). A 12-pack is $5.25. What's the better price? Have students work in pairs to decide which is the better price in each of the six pairs illustrated. Ask pairs to share their responses with the whole class.

3. Continue with part B. Ask students to indicate the price of the items illustrated. Go over the items with them, writing the total prices on the board or overhead transparency.

4. Have students, in pairs or triads, look in newspapers or magazines, cut out products, paste them on some paper, and create a problem as in part B. Show them how to indicate the total number and the individual or unit price. Ask them to share their papers with another group, who will calculate the total price. When papers have been returned to the original groups, go over the problems to see if calculations are correct. Post the work around the room.

## Practice:  Need

**Materials needed:** student book, page 14

1. Refer back to the need list students generated for Student Handout #10. Ask around the room, "Do you need (mention an item from the list)?" If a student answers "yes," repeat to the class, "He/She needs (item)." If a student answers "no," say "She/He doesn't need (item)." Do this several times to model use of the verb *to need*.

2. Use the Mini-Lesson box to illustrate the use of the target verb. Write other examples on the board or an overhead transparency.

3. Have students respond to the prompts in part A. What does Sam need? How much is it? What do Jim and Mary need? Do they need a new car? Do they need two lamps? How much are they? Continue with the rest of the section; then have students write out their responses.

4. In part B, have students change the statements to the negative, orally first and then in writing.

5. Distribute copies of Student Handout #11 for students to complete as an outside assignment. Process the exercises at the beginning of the next session.

## Read and Write

**Materials needed:** student book, page 15

1. Before they open their books, tell students they are going to read about a man who needs some things. First, however, they are going to make a few *guesses* as to who he is and what he needs. Ask them to write their answers to the following questions on a slip of paper so they may check them as they read.

(1) Is the man's name Robert, Steve, or Bill?

(2) Does he need things for his apartment, his work, or his car?

(3) Does he need furniture, tires, or a new desk?

(4) Does he need gas, food, or more money?

2. After they have noted their guesses, invite them to read along with you silently as you read the first paragraph aloud to them. What is the man's name? Does he need things for his apartment, his work, or his car?

3. Continue with the second paragraph in the same manner. Have students read the third paragraph silently; then ask them a few comprehension check questions. Invite student volunteers to finish the last paragraph. Check for comprehension.

4. Ask students to compare, in writing, the approximate prices of a few items from their "needs" list from Student Handout #10 or from the "shopping list" generated by the class in Oral Production, #1 (page 20). Ask them to look in magazines and newspapers or even visit some stores in the community to compare prices. Have them create a list of the products and the prices they found and then write about their findings, using the reading in this section as a model. Stress that creating the list is a very important step in the writing process and must be done before they begin to write. If you collect this assignment to assess, have students include all copies of their writing—list, rough draft, subsequent drafts, and final copy.

# Check Your Understanding

**Materials needed:** Student Handout #12; newspaper ads

1. The assessment for this unit is in two parts. You will administer the first part individually. It consists of questions that the students answer orally. You will ask each student up to five of the following questions (or create your own) and rate each response +, O, or –. A "+" indicates very good mastery of the terms, an "O" is satisfactory/good, and a "–" is indicates more practice is needed. Rate responses on students' handouts; then let them continue the test. An acceptable level for continuing on to the next unit would be three out of five correct responses. If students don't attain the desired level of competence, allow them time to practice and try again.

(1) (Show student a can of soda, fruit, vegetables, etc.) How many ounces are there in this can?

(2) (Show student one of the pairs from page 13 of the student book, or make up your own.) Which one is the better price?

(3) (Show student an ad in the newspaper for a common product.) What's the price?

(4) (Show student an ad from the newspaper for food per pound.) If I want two pounds, what's the price?

(5) Tell me three things that you need.

(6) Tell me something that you don't need but you really want.

(7) (Point to a picture in the student book from this unit.) What do you need?

(8) Do you need a vacation? more money? a new car?

2. Allow students to finish the rest of the assessment on their own. Complete

sentences and perfect grammar are not the objective, nor is punctuation an issue at this point. Look for the ability to communicate ideas.

---

## Answer Key

### Student Handout #9—Multiples in Buying (page 25)

Answers will vary. Look for items that are typically bought in the numbers indicated. If the student can show you an ad for something in a unit not normally found, accept the answer, but explain that is not normally how that item is sold. The number of items in each column may vary depending on the likelihood of finding items sold in that multiple. Expect fewer items in the three and one-hundred columns.

### Student Handout #10—Needs and Wants (page 26)

Answers will vary.

### Student Handout #11—Using *Need* (page 27)

A. 1. Does she need a new refrigerator?

2. Do Mike and Mia (they) need some milk?

3. Does his brother (he) need a job?

4. Do I need to see a doctor?

5. Do we need a ride to school?

B. 1. No, they don't. They need a (soccer) ball.

2. No, she doesn't. She needs gas.

3. No, he doesn't. He needs water.

4. No, they don't. They need a soda (a drink, something to drink, etc.).

### Student Handout #12—Check Your Understanding (page 28)

A. See the teacher guide for this section.

B. 1. They don't need a new bed.

2. Sally doesn't need gas for her car.

3. Mike and I don't need a ride to work.

4. Don doesn't need new shoes.

5. We don't need a dozen eggs.

C. 1. Does she need help?

2. Do Joan and Mia need to study?

3. Does Albert need a new set of tires?

4. Do we need to clean the apartment?

5. Do you need a vacation?

D. Answers will vary. Accept any reasonable need or want. Look for the ability to distinguish between the two terms.

# 9.  Multiples in Buying

**Make a list of things you can buy in these numbers:**

| Each | Pair | Three |
|------|------|-------|
|      |      |       |

| Six | One Dozen | One Hundred |
|-----|-----------|-------------|
|     |           |             |

# 10. Needs and Wants

**Write at least 10 things you need and at least 10 things you really want but don't need:**

| Things I really need | Things I really want |
|---|---|
|  |  |

# 11. Using *Need*

**A. Change each sentence to a question:**

1. She needs a new refrigerator. _________________________________

2. Mike and Mia need some milk. _________________________________

3. His brother needs a job. _________________________________

4. I need to see the doctor. _________________________________

5. We need a ride to school. _________________________________

**B. Look at the picture and answer the question:**

*Example:*

Does Sam need money?

*No, he doesn't. He needs new shoes.*

1. Do these soccer players need shoes?

_________________________________

2. Does Kim need a car?

_________________________________

3. Does he need a glass?

_________________________________

4. Do they need food?

_________________________________

# 12. Check Your Understanding

**A. Answer the questions the teacher asks you.**

  + = very good   O = good   – = need more practice

  1. _________   2. _________   3. _________   4. _________   5. _________

**B. Write a negative sentence using *need*:**

1. They / a new bed ____________________________________________________

2. Sally / gas for her car ____________________________________________

3. Mike and I / a ride to work ________________________________________

4. Don / new shoes ____________________________________________________

5. We / a dozen eggs __________________________________________________

**C. Write a question using *need*:**

1. she / help ________________________________________________________

2. Joan and Mia / to study tonight ____________________________________

3. Albert / a new set of tires ________________________________________

4. we / to clean the apartment ________________________________________

5. you / a vacation __________________________________________________

**D. Make a list of at least five things you need. Make another list of at least five things you don't need but you really want:**

| Things I need | Things I want but don't need |
| --- | --- |
| 1. ____________________ | 1. ____________________ |
| 2. ____________________ | 2. ____________________ |
| 3. ____________________ | 3. ____________________ |
| 4. ____________________ | 4. ____________________ |
| 5. ____________________ | 5. ____________________ |

# COLORS AND SHAPES



## Vocabulary Input

**Materials needed:** student book, page 16; large cutouts of shapes; flash cards with patterns (one with stripes, one with checks, etc.); marking pens of target colors; five chairs of different colors (borrow from other classrooms); poster or butcher paper

1. Use the colored pens to introduce the colors. Pick up a pen, a blue pen, for example. Say, "Pick up the blue pen. Drop the blue pen. Pick up the blue pen . . .," each time modeling the action. Play catch with the pen with some of the students. Give the pen to one of the students. Say, "Who has the blue pen? Point to the person with the blue pen . . ." Do this with several colors until all colors have been introduced.

2. Place the five colored chairs in a row in front of the class. Hold up one of the colored pens, perhaps a red one. Model and say, "Put the red pen on the blue chair." With another pen say, "Put the green pen under the brown chair." Continue doing this; then ask students to perform the task. Ask, "Is the red pen on the blue chair?" (Yes) "Is the green pen under the blue chair?" (No). Have students stand in front of a colored chair. Mix in terms like *next to, behind, on*, always referring to a colored chair or pen. (*Note:* If colored chairs are not available, you might place a piece of colored paper on each chair to "color" them.)

3. Introduce the shapes in the same manner; place them on, under, next to, in front of, and behind the colored chairs. ("Put the triangle in front of the green chair.") You can also introduce the patterns (stripes, solids, checks) in the same way, using the flash cards as the manipulatives. Always model first, and then ask students to perform. Allow students to command you and each other when they are ready to vocalize the commands.

4. Use the illustrations on page 16 of the student book to reinforce the shapes and patterns just introduced. Ask them to point to, touch, put their finger on, etc., each shape or pattern. Use the position of the shapes to reinforce terms like *next to, between*, and *on the right of*.

5. Have students, per your instructions, draw colored lines, squares, dark circles, light triangles, etc., on a sheet of paper while you model for them on poster or butcher paper. Use terms such as *above, under, between, next to, on the right of*, and *on the left of*. Repeat the activity, this time without modeling for them. Have them compare their completed paper with others in the class.

6. On a large piece of poster or butcher paper, write the names of the colors using their respective colored pen (red in red pen, etc.). Write the names of the shapes with a drawing beside each

(a square next to the word *square*, some stripes next to *stripes*, etc.). Display the poster in the room for the duration of the classes. (They can refer to the chart in a later unit on clothing).

## Oral Production

**Materials needed:** student book, page 17; examples of art (from books, slides, posters, and other sources) that utilize geometric shapes, lines, checks, stripes, etc.; various examples of artwork representing different styles and genres (impressionist, landscapes, portraits, etc.)

1. Begin by standing next to one of the students closest to you. Nudge the student and ask, "Who is that man over there? The man in the (describe the color of another student's shirt). And who is that woman over there (indicate a woman on the other side of the room)? The woman with the (describe the color of her shoes)." Ask about a few other students in the class in the same way. (Don't be afraid to "ham it up" a little—the students will love it!)

2. Direct student attention to the picture in part A. Have students cover the text with a piece of paper. Ask them who they think the people are in the picture. What do they think they are doing? Have them guess, even though they don't really know what the conversation is about. The idea is to get them to create some kind of context for the listening, based on what they see in the picture.

3. Read the first dialogue to the students, varying your voice to indicate a change in speakers, while students are still covering the text. Have students point to the person in the picture that the dialogue is referring to. Read the dialogue again, this time as students read along silently. Ask a few comprehension check questions.

4. Follow the same sequence for the dialogue in part B. After reading the conversation, ask students if they like that kind of art. Show them examples of other art genres. Describe, using colors and other key words, the pieces you share with them. Ask them to describe what they see in the paintings. Always model for them the correct placement of the adjective, but don't overtly correct any errors in syntax they may make.

5. Ask students to work in pairs to describe to each other what they see in each of the four illustrations in part C.

6. Ask students, in their pairs, to describe objects around the room. One student will begin by describing an object by its size, shape, and color. His or her partner will then guess what the first student is describing. Once the object is guessed, partners change roles; the second student describes, and the first student guesses.

# Shapes and Patterns in Your World

**Materials needed:** student book, page 18; magazines and newspapers; Student Handout #13

1. Explain to your students that when they learn something new, they need to connect it to what they already know. They should try to make it fit into their context. The Think! box at the top of page 18 refers to this concept.

2. Have students look around the room and point to any circles they can find. Point to the clock on the wall. What is it? Is it a square? Is it a diamond? Is it an oval? Is it a circle? Have them name or point to anything square in the room. Do this for other shapes and patterns.

3. Refer students to the illustration on page 18 of the student book. Have them point to, touch, show you, etc., the assorted shapes and patterns on the shelves in the store. What about in nature? Discuss some of the shapes and patterns that are found in the insect world, in fruit, in other plants.

4. Have students look in magazines to find pictures that show some of the shapes and patterns you have been discussing. This activity can be extended to include cutting examples of different shapes and making class posters of the examples the students find—a poster with triangles, a poster with squares, etc. Have students label the object they include on the poster.

5. Distribute copies of Student Handout #13. Have students list, and indicate the color of, as many things as they can see in the room that fit into any one of the shape or pattern categories. An object may be included in more than one column. Process the activity by having students share a few of their responses with the whole class. If the handout is assigned as an outside activity, they may list things they find in their home.

# Practice: Adjectives

**Materials needed:** student book, page 19; Student Handouts #13 and #14

1. Use student responses to Student Handout #13 to illustrate the use of adjectives and their placement in relation to the noun they are describing. Point out that in English we usually place the descriptor in front of the noun it describes (*white floor tile; red, white, and blue flag*). Ask students to check their responses to see if they did, in fact, place the color in front of the object being described.

2. Use the Mini-Lesson on page 19 to show how the adjective is placed in relation to the noun and when coupled with the verb *to be*. Point out that numbers or words that limit will come before the word they describe.

3. In part A, have students, in pairs, describe to each other the items

illustrated, using the descriptors listed below each picture. Model for them, placing the adjective before the noun: "orange bicycles." Note that some students may try to create a plural form of the descriptor ("oranges bicycles")—a common form in other languages. Simply model the correct form again. Avoid overt correction. (Be careful with "hot cup of coffee," meaning "cup of hot coffee." Is the cup hot, or is the coffee hot?)

4. Continue with part B, in which the adjective is placed after the noun and separated from the noun by the verb *to be*: "The water is cold." Ask students if there is another way to express the same idea ("It's cold water.").

5. Distribute copies of Student Handout #14 for students to complete as independent practice. Review the exercises at the beginning of the next session.

~~~~~~~~~~~~~~~~~~~~~~~~~~~~~~~~~~~~~~~~~~~~~~

# Read and Write

**Materials needed:** student book, page 20; Student Handout #15; pictures of colors in nature (autumn leaves, ocean underwater scenes, etc.); overhead transparencies or poster paper

1. Begin by showing students pictures of colorful nature scenes—fish, butterflies, autumn leaves, sunrise/sunset scenes—anything with lots of color. Ask students to identify the colors they see in the pictures. As they name some of the colors, repeat back to them what they identify, expanding on what they say and modeling the correct syntax. For example, if a student says, "Orange," you respond, "That's right. There are orange leaves falling from the trees." Pass out pictures to small groups and have them identify items and colors in them. They can do this orally or create a written list to share with the whole class.

2. Direct student attention to the pictures on page 20 of the student book. Ask

students what color apples, oranges, and lemons are and what color tomatoes and grapes are. What color is lettuce? the sky?

3. Begin reading the first paragraph aloud to the class, while students follow in the text. As you continue through the reading, stop and ask a few comprehension questions to be sure students are understanding the text.

4. When finished with the reading, distribute copies of Student Handout #15. Model for students the use of a cluster map by doing one for them on an overhead transparency or on poster paper. Choose a picture that they have been looking at and begin to note some of the colors and shapes you and they see in it. Include the topic in a main circle, then objects with their colors and shapes in the subcircles:
~~~~~~~~~~~~~~~~~~~~~~~~~~~~~~~~~~~~~~~~~~~~~~

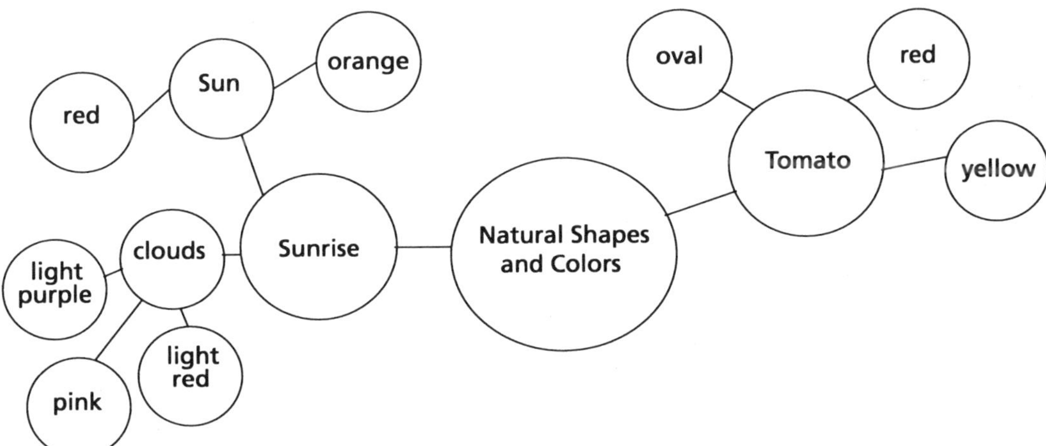


Ask students to create their own cluster map based on a picture you give them or one they find on their own. On the handout, they don't have to use all the circles, or they may add others as needed. The diagram is meant only as a model. It can take on any form, dictated by the topic. Show them that now they have an idea bank from which they can begin to organize their writing. Ask them to write about the colors and shapes they encounter in their own world, using the reading as a model.

## Check Your Understanding

**Materials needed:** Student Handout #12; newspaper ads

1. The assessment for this unit is in two parts. You will administer the first section individually. It consists of questions that the students answer orally. You will ask each student up to five of the following questions (or create your own) and rate each response +, O, or –. A "+" indicates very good mastery of the terms, an "O" is satisfactory / good, and a "–" indicates more practice is needed. Rate responses on students' handouts; then let them continue the test. An acceptable level for continuing on to the next unit would be three out of five correct responses. If students don't attain the desired level of competence, allow them time to practice and try again.

   (1) (Show student a shape on a flash card.) What shape is this?

   (2) (Show student one of the colors targeted.) What color is this?

   (3) (Show student a pattern from the unit.) What is this?

   (4) (Show student a picture from the newspaper with lots of different colors.) What colors do you see?

   (5) (Show student a picture, label, ad, etc.) What shapes do you see?

   (6) What is square (round, oval, diamond etc.) in this classroom?

(7) (Show student a multicolored object with a distinctive shape.) Describe this to me.

2. Allow students to finish the rest of the assessment on their own. Complete

sentences and perfect grammar are not the objective, nor is punctuation an issue at this point. Look for the ability to communicate ideas.

---

## Answer Key

### Student Handout #13—Shapes and Patterns in Your World (page 35)

Answers will vary depending on where the students do the activity.

### Student Handout #14—Using Adjectives (page 36)

A. 1. Those are blue pencils.

2. They are good books.

3. It's a cold soda.

4. It's a clean apartment.

5. Those are beautiful mountains.

B. 1. The cars are red and white.

2. My brothers are tall.

3. The soccer games are exciting.

4. Those houses are yellow.

5. These green trees are tall.

C. 1. Mike has long, brown wavy (wavy, long brown) hair.

2. Sheila has a small red motorcycle.

3. They live in a pretty green house.

4. Ron drives a large blue truck.

5. I'm wearing a yellow striped T-shirt.

6. They have good chocolate ice cream.

### Student Handout #15—Cluster Map (page 37)

Answers will vary.

### Student Handout #16—Check Your Understanding (page 38)

A. See the teacher guide for this section.

B. 1. Frank has a big black car.

2. Sandra lives in a green house.

3. We want a cup of hot tea.

4. The movie is funny.

5. It's a green striped chair.

C. 1. These are fast cars.

2. Those are big black cats.

3. They want red apples.

4. Those are large trucks.

5. We have good friends.

D. Answers will vary. Focus on the use of the target terms (colors and shapes) and correct use of adjectives and their placement.

# 13.  Shapes and Patterns in Your World

**Find objects around you that have one of these shapes or patterns. Then list the objects and their colors:**

| Squares | Circles | Triangles | Ovals | Diamonds |
|---|---|---|---|---|
| *White floor tile* | | | | |

| Checks | Stripes | Solid | Dark | Light |
|---|---|---|---|---|
| | *Red, white, and blue flag* | | | |

   **35**  *Life Themes for ESL Classes:  You and Your Money – 1*

# 14. Using Adjectives

**A. Change each sentence as in the example:**

*Example:*   The dog is big.  ___*It's a big dog.*___________________________

1.  Those pencils are blue.  _______________________________________

2.  The books are good.  _________________________________________

3.  The soda is cold.  ___________________________________________

4.  The apartment is clean.  ______________________________________

5.  Those mountains are beautiful.  _________________________________

**B. Change each sentence to the plural:**

*Example:*   That chair is blue.  ___*Those chairs are blue.*________________

1.  The car is red and white.  _____________________________________

2.  My brother is tall.  __________________________________________

3.  The soccer game is exciting.  ___________________________________

4.  That house is yellow.  ________________________________________

5.  This green tree is tall.  _______________________________________

**C. Combine the sentences into one:**

*Example*:   She has a dog. It's black. It's big.  ___*She has a big black dog.*___

1.  Mike has long hair. It's brown. It's wavy.  _______________________

2.  Sheila has a motorcycle. It's small. It's red.  _____________________

3.  They live in a house. It's pretty. It's green.  _____________________

4.  Ron drives a truck. It's large. It's blue.  ________________________

5.  I'm wearing a T-shirt. It's striped. It's yellow.  ___________________

6.  They have ice cream. It's chocolate. It's good.  ___________________

    *36*   *Life Themes for ESL Classes: You and Your Money – 1*

# 15. Cluster Map

**Follow your teacher's instructions to fill in this cluster map:**

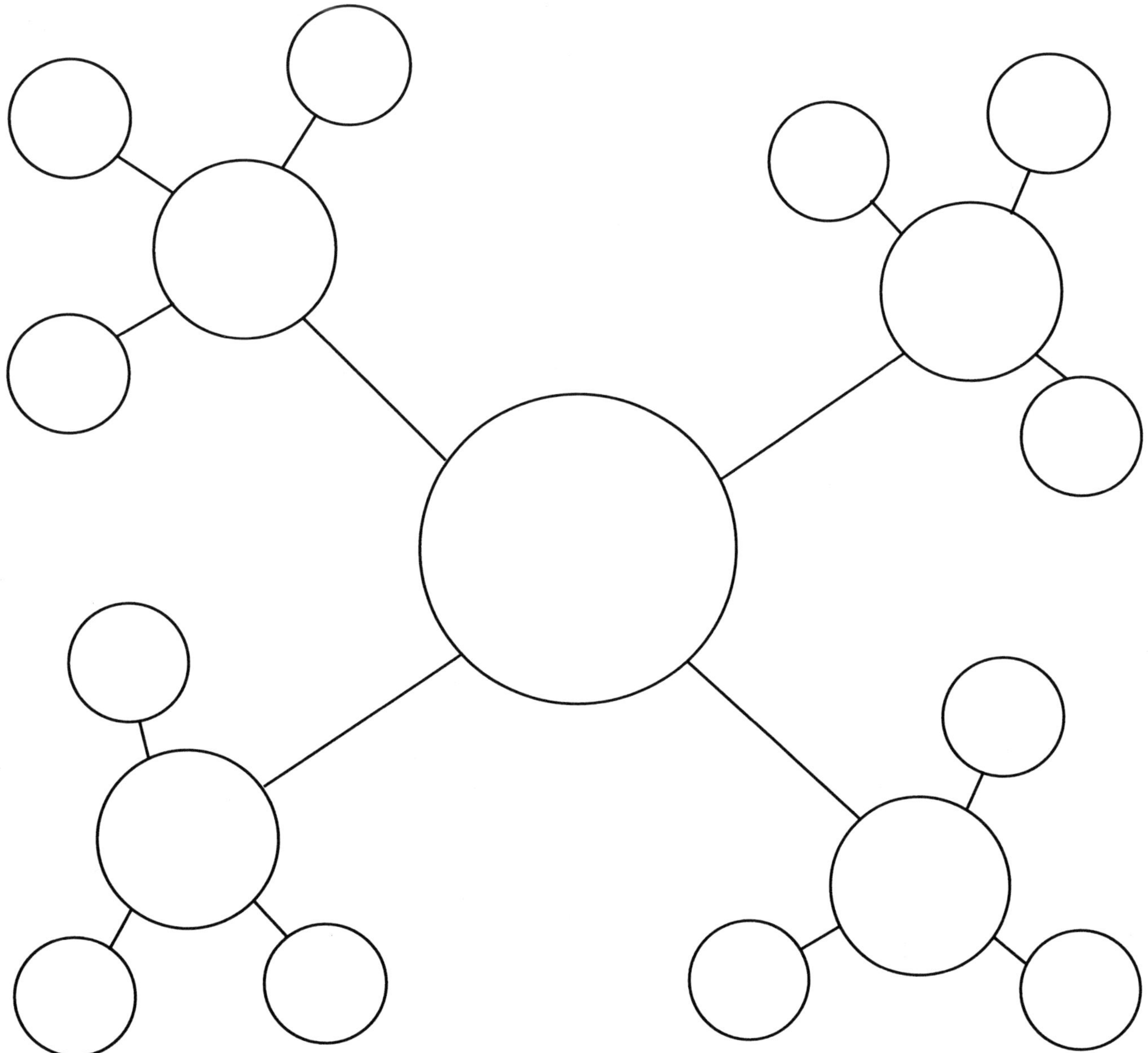

# 16. Check Your Understanding

**A. Answer the questions the teacher asks you.**

+ = very good   **O** = good   – = need more practice

1. _________   2. _________   3. _________   4. _________   5. _________

**B. Write a sentence with the words:**

1. Frank / has / car / black / big ________________________________________

2. Sandra / lives / house / green ________________________________________

3. We / want / cup of tea / hot________________________________________

4. The / funny / movie ________________________________________

5. It's / chair / striped / green ________________________________________

**C. Change to the plural:**

1. This is a fast car. ________________________________________

2. That is a big black cat. ________________________________________

3. They want a red apple. ________________________________________

4. That is a large truck. ________________________________________

5. We have a good friend. ________________________________________

**D. Write a description of something in nature** (a mountain, a sunrise or sunset—something with shapes and colors):

________________________________________

________________________________________

________________________________________

________________________________________

________________________________________

________________________________________

________________________________________

   *38*   *Life Themes for ESL Classes: You and Your Money – 1*

# CLOTHES



**Materials needed:** student book, page 21; articles of used clothing; old magazines; Student Handout #17; folders, cardboard barriers, etc., to separate students

1. Begin by showing students an article of clothing that you have brought into the classroom. Say and model, "Point to the blue pants. Take the blue pants. (Give the article to a student.) Who has the blue pants? Give the blue pants to him / her." Do this until you have introduced several articles of clothing; then ask who has what clothing. Point to a student and ask the class if he or she has the blue pants. Ask another if he or she has the blue pants or the green shirt, etc.

2. Describe what you are wearing, head to toe, including colors and patterns (stripes, solids, checks, etc.). Describe a few other students in the class who are wearing different clothing.

3. Use page 21 of the student book to introduce other articles of clothing not found in the room. Use TPR (Total Physical Response) techniques to reinforce the terms. Have students point to, touch, show, or put their finger on each of the items as you model for them.

4. Look around the room to review who is wearing what. Then, without looking directly at the person, tell students that you are thinking of someone in the class. Tell students that they can guess who you are thinking of only by asking if the person is wearing an article of clothing, naming the color or pattern. Write on the board the question "Is the person wearing _____________?" Model a few questions for them: "Is the person wearing black shoes?" "Is the person wearing a yellow blouse?" Begin asking volunteers to ask questions. Answer only questions referring to clothes and colors or patterns. If a student's first question is answered "yes," he or she may guess whom you are thinking of. If the student guesses correctly, invite that student to the front of the class to think of another classmate and answer the next round of questions.

5. Make copies of Student Handout #17. Cut each copy in half, separating part A from part B. Ask students to form pairs and sit facing their partner. Pass out part A to one partner and part B to the other. Make sure they do not let each other see their copy. Ask them to create a visual barrier with a book, notebook, manila folder, or a piece of cardboard. Demonstrate to them that part A and part B are both missing some of the items. Their goal is to make their sheets the same. They need to talk to each other to identify the items that are missing. They will then draw in the missing items. They will write names of the items under the pictures. When they have finished, ask them to compare their sheets to make sure they are the same.

## Oral Production

**Materials needed:**  student book, page 22; Student Handout #18

1. Direct student attention to the Think! box on page 22. Ask students to look at the pictures before they listen to or look at the conversation (it's usually best to have students cover the text with paper). Have them predict what the selection will be about in order to be more focused listeners. Record some of their predictions on the board or a transparency. Continue displaying the predictions during the activity.

2. Read the conversation in part A for students, varying your voice to indicate a change in speakers. When finished, ask a few comprehension questions to make sure they understood most of what they heard. Begin to use the simple future tense in your questions: "Where are they going to go tonight?" "What is Mike going to wear to the party?" "Is Lan going to wear a red blouse?" Ask a few volunteers to read the parts for the class.

3. Continue with the conversation in part B in the same manner, asking comprehension questions afterwards.

4. Invite students to practice dialogues A and B in pairs. Make sure they switch roles to practice all forms. Have them remain in pairs and practice saying what they are going to wear, using part C as a guide.

5. Distribute copies of Student Handout #18, a people search about clothing. Have students ask the question "Are you going to wear . . .?" to find out what people are going to wear tomorrow. When they find someone who fits a description, have them get that person to sign their paper on the appropriate line. They may obtain the signature of a person only twice. When they have filled their sheet with signatures, ask them to choose eight people to write a sentence about ("Miko is going to wear a dress tomorrow.").

## What Are You Going to Pack?

**Materials needed:**  an old suitcase; used clothing from Vocabulary Input, page 39; student book, page 23; a map of the United States; poster paper

1. Place an old suitcase on a table in front of the room. Hold it up and ask students to point to the suitcase. Pass the suitcase around the room, using TPR to reinforce the term. Show students the clothes you have. Review for them the different clothes. Tell students you are going to go on a trip to another city. You are going to take some extra clothes with you. Show them one article of clothing, fold it, and put it into the suitcase, saying, "I'm going to pack my ______." Invite other students to help you pack.

2. Go over the terms illustrated at the top of page 23 of the student book. Use TPR to introduce those items that are new. Ask students if the item is something to wear when it's hot, or when it's cold outside.

3. Show students a map of the United States. Point out the location of Florida (or another warm climate location if you are in Florida). Ask them if they think it's hot or cold in Florida during the time of year you are in. Tell them they are going to pack their suitcases for a trip to that warm climate. What are they going to pack? Are they going to need a jacket? mittens? a robe? a sweater? a swimsuit? Inside the suitcase in part A, have students make a list of the clothes that they think they are going to need on a trip to a warm climate. Have them continue with part B in the same manner, only this time packing for a trip where the weather is very cold. Process both sections by creating a class "suit-case" on poster paper. Record student responses by asking individuals to share new ideas only; that is, ask them to share what they have packed that has not been "packed" in the class suitcase. Display the poster in the room.

## Practice: *Going To*

**Materials needed:** student book, page 24; Student Handout #19

1. Begin by modeling a few commands for the class: "Stand. Walk to the door. Open the door. Run to your desk. Sit." Do the actions. As you are performing the tasks, ask students what you are doing: "What am I doing? Am I sitting? Am I closing the door?" After doing the actions, say the commands again. This time, before you perform the task, tell the class, "I'm going to stand. I'm going to walk to the door. I'm going to open (close) the door. I'm going to run to my desk and I'm going to sit. What am I going to do?" Listen for responses. Don't overtly correct errors; just repeat the phrase again, modeling the correct form. Continue using other commands and having individuals perform the tasks while the rest tell you what each student "is going to do."

2. Focus student attention on page 24 of the student book. Using the Mini-Lesson as a guide, show how the simple future tense is formed using *going to*. Have students look at the pictures. What is going to happen in each picture? What are the people going to do? Point to each picture and ask a question requiring a yes or no answer: "Am I going to drink?" "Am I going to eat?" "Is she going to ride a bicycle at the beach?" "Is she going to run in the park?" Invite students to form pairs and practice saying to each other what they see is going to happen in each illustration. When they finish, have them write a sentence for each. Have them also ask each other questions such as "What are you going to do tonight? tomorrow? Saturday night? this weekend?"

3. Tell students that they are going to see into the future. They are going to predict what three people in the class are going to do or be 10 years from now. Model a few ideas for them: "Let's see. In 10 years, Mohammad is going to be an engineer for a large company. In

10 years, he's going to be married. He's going to have three children." Have students choose which three people they are going to write about, but not tell anyone who they are. Ask them to write out their predictions. Collect the predictions and read them to the class without saying any names (be sure to screen out anything that may be sensi-

tive). Have the class guess who the prediction is for.

4. Distribute copies of Student Handout #19 to be completed as an outside assignment. Have students complete the activities as directed. Process the exercises at the beginning of the next session.

# Read and Write

**Materials needed:** student book, page 25; world map; travel brochures for different world destinations; geography books (lower grade level)

1. Direct student attention to the Think! box on page 25 of the student book. Remind students that predicting what they are going to read will help them understand what they are reading. Have them look at the first two pictures in part A and guess what the reading is about. What are the animals in the first picture? (kangaroos) Where do we find them in the world? Show them a map of the world and ask if anyone can show you where Australia is. Once Australia has been identified, let students know that Australia is the only place in the world where you can find kangaroos that are not in zoos. Knowing that, where, then, is the couple going to travel? (first picture) What are they going to pack? (second picture)

2. Have students read the first two paragraphs, either silently or aloud. Ask a few comprehension questions to check understanding. Ask students to look at the last two pictures and again predict what is going to happen in the reading. After reading the third paragraph with students, pause and explain that Australia is in the Southern Hemisphere, where summer is from December through February and winter is June, July, and August. Ask any students from a country in the Southern Hemisphere if that is the case. Continue with the final paragraph.

3. For part B, ask students to imagine that they are going to travel to another part of the world. They are going to pack their suitcases for the trip, so they need to decide what they are going to pack. Where are they going to go? Have them ask themselves the questions listed. They should make a list of things to pack based on what they are going to do when they get there. You may want to give them access to travel brochures (easily obtained from a friendly travel agent) or some simple geography books. Have them predict the climate based on hemisphere, time of year, altitude, etc. They will then write a short piece about their pending trip that will include the above information.

# Check Your Understanding

**Materials needed:** Student Handout #20

1. The assessment for this unit is in two parts. You will administer the first part individually. It consists of questions that the students answer orally. You will ask each student up to five of the following questions (or create your own) and rate each response +, O, or –. A "+" indicates very good mastery of the terms, an "O" is satisfactory / good, and a "–" indicates more practice is needed. Rate students' responses on their handouts; then let them continue the test. An acceptable level for continuing on to the next unit would be three out of five correct responses. If students don't attain the desired level of competence, allow them time to practice and try again.

    (1) (Show student an article of clothing.) What is this?

    (2) (Show student a clothing accessory.) What is this?

    (3) What are you wearing today?

    (4) What are you going to wear tomorrow?

    (5) What are you going to do this Saturday night?

    (6) Show pictures from page 24 of the student book.) What is going to happen?

    (7) (Give a command.) What are you going to do? Repeat with several commands.

    (8) If you travel to your home country, what are you going to pack in your suitcase?

2. Allow students to finish the rest of the assessment on their own. Complete sentences and perfect grammar are not the objective, nor is punctuation an issue at this point. Look for the ability to communicate ideas.

---

## *Answer Key*

### Student Handout #17—Back and Forth (page 45)

| | |
|---|---|
| 1. tie | 9. boots |
| 2. socks | 10. gloves |
| 3. belt | 11. pants |
| 4. blouse | 12. skirt |
| 5. umbrella | 13. coat |
| 6. sweater | 14. watch |
| 7. suit | 15. necklace |
| 8. jacket | |

Check to make sure that students have correctly identified all items that were missing from their sheet:

### Student Handout #18—People Search (page 46)

Answers will vary. Check by processing together orally as a whole class. Ask students to identify the people they have listed. Then check with the person identified to verify that in fact he or she is going to wear that item tomorrow.

## Student Handout #19—Using *Going To* (page 47)

A. 1. He's going to watch a movie.

2. She's going to read a book.

3. They're going to eat in a restaurant.

4. They're going to buy food (in a super-market).

5. He's going to wash clothes.

6. She's going to talk on the phone.

B. 1. She's going to play volleyball tomor-row.

2. They're going to clean their house tomorrow.

3. I'm going to wear a green coat tomorrow.

4. We're going to stay home and rest tomorrow.

5. Truong is going to buy clothes tomor-row.

## Student Handout #20—Check Your Understanding (page 48)

A. See the teacher guide for this section.

B. 1. She is (She's) going to shop at the mall.

2. He is (He's) going to watch television.

3. We are (We're) going to swim at the beach.

4. It is (It's) going to rain.

5. I am (I'm) going to stay home.

C. 1. They are (They're) going to wear sweaters.

2. She is (She's) going to wear a dress.

3. He is (He's) going to wear a tie.

4. They are (They're) going to wear hats.

D. Answers will vary. Look for correct use of the simple future tense and inclusion of articles of clothing.

# 17. Back and Forth

**A.**

1. 
________

2. 
________

3. 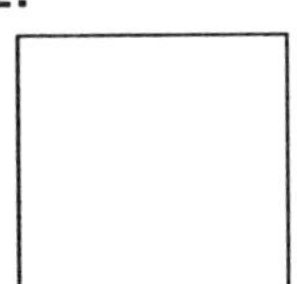
________

4. 
________

5. 
________

6. 
________

7. 
________

8. 
________

9. 
________

10. 
________

11. 
________

12. 
________

13. 
________

14. 
________

15. 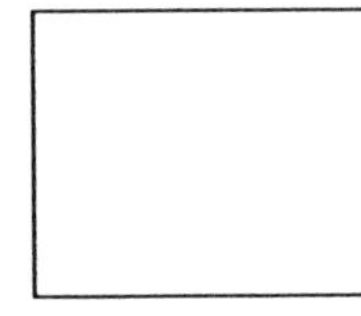
________

**B.**

1. 
________

2. 
________

3. 
________

4. 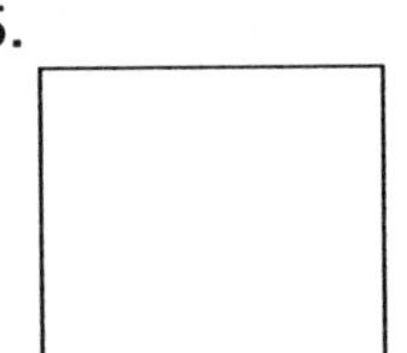
________

5. 
________

6. 
________

7. 
________

8. 
________

9. 
________

10. 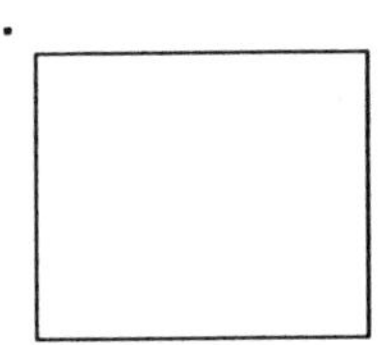
________

11. 
________

12. 
________

13. 
________

14. 
________

15. 
________

# 18.  People Search

**Find someone who is going to wear . . .**

blue pants tomorrow. _______________________________________________________

a green shirt tomorrow. ____________________________________________________

a white blouse tomorrow. ___________________________________________________

a black or brown skirt tomorrow. ___________________________________________

a white shirt tomorrow. ____________________________________________________

a necklace tomorrow. _______________________________________________________

black socks tomorrow. ______________________________________________________

white socks tomorrow. ______________________________________________________

a brown belt tomorrow. _____________________________________________________

a dark suit tomorrow. ______________________________________________________

a gold watch tomorrow. _____________________________________________________

a ring tomorrow. ___________________________________________________________

black pants tomorrow. ______________________________________________________

a blue shirt tomorrow. _____________________________________________________

glasses tomorrow. __________________________________________________________

a tie tomorrow. ____________________________________________________________

a hat tomorrow. ____________________________________________________________

a dress tomorrow. __________________________________________________________

blue jeans tomorrow. _______________________________________________________

   *46   Life Themes for ESL Classes: You and Your Money – 1*

# 19. Using *Going To*

**A. Look at the picture. Write a sentence using *going to*:**

1. ______________________________________________

2. ______________________________________________

3. ______________________________________________

4. ______________________________________________

5. ______________________________________________

6. ______________________________________________

**B. Change to the future using *tomorrow*:**

*Example:*   He's watching TV.   *He's going to watch TV tomorrow.*

1. She's playing volleyball. ______________________________________________

2. They're cleaning their house. ______________________________________________

3. I'm wearing a green coat. ______________________________________________

4. We're staying home and resting. ______________________________________________

5. Truong is buying clothes. ______________________________________________

   *47   Life Themes for ESL Classes: You and Your Money – 1*

# 20. Check Your Understanding

**A. Answer the questions the teacher asks you.**

+ = very good   **O** = good   – = need more practice

1. _________  2. _________  3. _________  4. _________  5. _________

**B. Change to the future:**

1. She is shopping at the mall. _______________________________________

2. He's watching television. _______________________________________

3. We're swimming at the beach. _______________________________________

4. It's raining. _______________________________________

5. I'm staying home. _______________________________________

**C. Look at the picture. What are they going to wear?**

1. _______________________________________

2. _______________________________________

3. _______________________________________

4. _______________________________________

**D. Write about your plans for this weekend.** (What are you going to do on Friday night, Saturday, Saturday night, and Sunday? What are you going to wear?) **Write your plans on the back of this paper.**

   **48**   *Life Themes for ESL Classes: You and Your Money – 1*

# PERSONAL FINANCE

## Vocabulary Input

**Materials needed:** samples of currency (real or play money); some canceled checks (or facsimiles); old bank savings passbook or statement; examples of credit cards; student book, page 26

1. Using some of the samples that you are able to bring into the classroom, introduce as many of the target terms as you can. Use TPR (pick up, point to, pass, put on the table, give to . . ., etc.) to create context. Ask students if they have or know someone who has a credit card, checking account, or savings account. Talk to them about the different parts of a check and what each part means: "What is the date? Who is writing the check? Who is the check for? How much is the check worth?" Show that the amount is written in numbers but also spelled out. Please note that care should be taken not to leave bank account and credit card numbers lying around. Use your own discretion in sharing that information.

2. Use the illustrations on page 26 of student book to support what you began with the samples. Students can also use the illustrations for reference later in this unit.

3. Review the spelling of numbers (given at the beginning of this book). Remind students of the use of hyphens for numbers past twenty. Have them practice writing several numbers as you dictate them.

4. Ask students when they use cash. When does one use checks? When do you need a loan? Where can you go to open a savings account? Explain that there are many kinds of money institutions (banks, savings and loan associations, loan companies, credit card companies, credit unions). At this point just make them aware that there are many different kinds of institutions.

## Oral Production

**Materials needed:** student book, page 27; Student Handout #21; poster paper

1. Have students, in pairs, look at the picture next to the conversation in part A on page 27 of the student book, while they cover the text with a piece of paper. Ask them to write at least two predictions about the conversation's content. What are the men going to talk about? Ask one pair to share their predictions with the class. Ask the rest of the class if they agree. Note any other opinions.

2.  While students still have the text of the conversation covered, read it for them. Pause along the way if you read something that agrees or disagrees with the class predictions. Ask a few comprehension check questions after you finish. Read the dialogue again, this time as students follow along in the text. Have other students read a part for the class.

3.  Continue with the second dialogue in the same manner. When finished, ask students to practice the dialogues in their pairs, changing roles to practice both questions and answers.

4.  In their pairs, have students create their own dialogue to present to the class.

5.  Distribute copies of Student Handout #21. Ask students to list things for which they pay cash. Elicit a few examples from the class. Then ask them to list things for which they might pay by check. Is it all right to buy a soda (or some other small item) with a check? List those things they might buy with a credit card and those large items they might buy with a loan. Allow less-experienced students to draw the item or cut and paste from magazines to identify some of the items they don't yet know how to say or write. Process the activity by having students share their responses with a partner to see what they had in common and then share with the whole class. Create a class poster of the results.

## Writing a Check

**Materials needed:** student book, pages 27 and 28; Student Handout #22; old canceled checks for reference

1.  Remind students of the dialogue in part B on page 27. Zineta is going to pay for the sofa by writing a check. How much does the sofa cost? Whom does Zineta have to pay?

2.  Direct student attention to the check at the top of page 28. Who is Bekir? Why is his name on the check with Zineta's name? What is her last name? Where does Zineta live? What's her phone number? Continue to ask questions about the check.

3.  Show students a few of your canceled checks. Have them identify some of the important information—amount, paid to, signature, etc.

4.  Have students look at the checks in part B. Ask a few questions about the first check. Who wrote the check? Who gets the money? How much? Divide students into triads and have them look at the rest of the checks and try to identify who the check is for, the amount, who is writing the check, and other information.

5.  Distribute copies of Student Handout #22. Have students, still in their triads, help each other fill in the checks with the information provided under each check. Model for them how to fill in the first check; then ask them to fill in the rest in the same way. As they are working on filling in the information, circulate to check for their understanding. If they are having difficulty, walk them through one more check as a model.

# Practice: *Going To*

**Materials needed:** student book, page 29; Student Handout #23

1. Begin by writing the names of five students on one side of the board or a transparency. On the other side, write five activities using the simple future *going to*:

   Juan     is going to write a letter.

   Tina     is going to buy a house.

   As in "detective" activities in earlier books in this series (*You and Your Life*, *You and Your Community*), tell students that you have selected only one combination to be the correct one. Give them a few examples by combining one of the names you have written and one of the actions. Students must form a question ("Is Juan going to buy a house?") in order to determine which is the "true" combination. Ask for questions from the class. Repeat each question, modeling the correct form for them without overt corrections; then answer the question. ("No, Juan isn't going to buy a house.")

Once a student gets a "yes" response from you, that person chooses the next new "correct" combination and fields the questions from the other students.

2. Direct student attention to the Mini-Lesson box at the top of page 29. Demonstrate the correct syntax for question formation and the inclusion of the contraction or *not* in the negative (no contraction is used in the first person singular when it's negative).

3. Have students form questions from the prompts in part A. Ask them to do this section orally first and then write out their responses.

4. Continue with part B by having students change the affirmative statements to the negative, orally first and then in writing.

5. Distribute copies of Student Handout #23. Have students complete the activity as an outside assignment. Process the activity at the beginning of the next session.

# Read and Write

**Materials needed:** student book, page 30

1. Begin by directing student attention to the Think! box at the top of page 30. Ask students to try to connect what they are reading to their own experiences. Is what is happening to the people in the reading also happening in their own life? If students can connect themselves in some way to the reading, it will be easier to comprehend and recall.

2. Have students look at the illustrations and predict what the reading is going to be about. In the first illustration, the people are filling out a form: "Why are they doing that? What are they asking

| I'm going to buy . . . | It's going to cost . . . | I'm going to pay for it by . . . |
| --- | --- | --- |
|  |  |  |

for? What do they need to have to buy a house? Do you ever borrow money?"

3. Begin reading the first paragraph with students. Ask if anyone has been to a bank. What's a bank like? Is it difficult to go there? Is it difficult to answer all the questions?

4. Have students read the three remaining paragraphs on their own, predicting first and then reading. After each paragraph, check for comprehension by discussing what the students have read.

5. Begin to discuss with students any plans they may have for buying something in the future. Suggest to them that they are probably going to buy some things for their home, some form of transportation (if they haven't already), and some personal items. Draw a large three-column chart on the overhead, board, or poster paper (see above).

Have students copy the chart on their own paper and then fill it in with information about some of the items they plan to purchase, how much they will cost, and how they plan to pay for them (cash, check, credit card, loan). Have students use this information to write a plan for their purchases, using the reading as a model.

## Check Your Understanding

**Materials Needed:** Student Handout #24

1. The assessment for this unit is in two parts. You will administer the first section individually. It consists of questions that the students answer orally. You will ask each student up to five of the following questions (or create your own) and rate each response +, O, or –. A "+" indicates very good mastery of the terms, an "O" is satisfactory / good, and a "–" indicates more practice is needed. Rate students' responses on their handouts; then let them continue the test. An acceptable level for continuing on to the next unit would be three out of five correct responses. If students don't attain the desired level of competence, allow them time to practice and try again.

Show student a filled in check:

(1) Who is this check for?

(2) How much is this check for?

(3) What is the date of the check?

(4) I'm going to buy a (mention a very inexpensive item). How can I pay for it?

(5) Are you going to school on Saturday night?

(6) Are you going to buy a car with cash?

(7) Are you going to buy a soda with a loan?

(8) Are you going to write a check for 50¢?

2. Allow students to finish the rest of the assessment on their own. Complete sentences and perfect grammar are not the objective, nor is punctuation an issue at this point. Look for the ability to communicate ideas.

---

## *Answer Key*

### Student Handout #21—How Will You Pay? (page 54)

Answers will vary. Look for appropriateness of the listed items in relation to how students might pay for them.

### Student Handout #22—Writing a Check (page 55)

Make sure the checks are filled out completely with current date, correct amount, correct spelling of numbers, and signature.

### Student Handout #23—Using *Going To* (page 56)

A. 1. No, she isn't. She's going to see a movie tomorrow.

2. No, they aren't. They're going to wash the car tomorrow.

3. No, he isn't. He's going to pay cash for the chair.

4. No, we aren't. We're going to pay for dinner with a (by) credit card.

5. No, she isn't. She's going to walk in the park on Saturday.

6. No, I'm not. I'm going to dance tonight.

### Student Handout #24—Check Your Understanding (page 57)

A. See the teacher guide for this section.

B. 1. Jim isn't going to play baseball.

2. She isn't going to buy a car.

3. We aren't going to pay cash.

4. They aren't going to see a friend.

5. It isn't going to snow tonight.

C. 1. Are you going to get a loan?

2. Is he going to see the doctor?

3. Are they going to run on Friday?

4. Is the movie going to end at five?

5. Are we going to have fun?

D. Look for effective use of the simple future tense and a basic grasp of methods of payment and personal finance.

# 21. How Will You Pay?

**Write the names of things you can buy with cash, check, credit card, or a loan:**

| Cash | Check |
|---|---|
| *a soda* | *food at the supermarket* |

| Credit Card | Loan |
|---|---|
| *clothes* | *a car* |

Name _________________________________________________  Date _________________________________

# 22.  Writing a Check

**Fill in the checks with the information under each one:**

| | |
|---|---|
| Name<br>Address<br>Phone<br><br>Pay to the<br>Order of ___________________  $ ______<br><br>________________________________ Dollars<br><br>For ____________  ____________ | Name<br>Address<br>Phone<br><br>Pay to the<br>Order of ___________________  $ ______<br><br>________________________________ Dollars<br><br>For ____________  ____________ |
| **Standard Gas Company  $25.00** | **Jensen's Department Store  $47.00** |
| Name<br>Address<br>Phone<br><br>Pay to the<br>Order of ___________________  $ ______<br><br>________________________________ Dollars<br><br>For ____________  ____________ | Name<br>Address<br>Phone<br><br>Pay to the<br>Order of ___________________  $ ______<br><br>________________________________ Dollars<br><br>For ____________  ____________ |
| **Olsen's Supermarket  $52.50** | **Valley Electric Company  $23.10** |
| Name<br>Address<br>Phone<br><br>Pay to the<br>Order of ___________________  $ ______<br><br>________________________________ Dollars<br><br>For ____________  ____________ | Name<br>Address<br>Phone<br><br>Pay to the<br>Order of ___________________  $ ______<br><br>________________________________ Dollars<br><br>For ____________  ____________ |
| **Mr. Mark Foster  $300.00** | **Dr. John Gray  $120.00** |
| Name<br>Address<br>Phone<br><br>Pay to the<br>Order of ___________________  $ ______<br><br>________________________________ Dollars<br><br>For ____________  ____________ | Name<br>Address<br>Phone<br><br>Pay to the<br>Order of ___________________  $ ______<br><br>________________________________ Dollars<br><br>For ____________  ____________ |
| **Max's Car Repair  $100.00** | **Valley Water Company  $45.00** |

# 23. Using *Going To*

**Look at each picture. Then answer the question:**

*Example*:

Is Jack going to drive his car to work tomorrow?   *No, he isn't.*
*He's going to ride his bicycle to work tomorrow.*

1. Is Nancy going to stay home tomorrow?   ___________________

___________________________________________________________

2. Are they going to wash their clothes tomorrow?   ___________

___________________________________________________________

3. Is he going to pay by check for the chair?   _______________

___________________________________________________________

4. Are we going to pay for dinner with cash?   ________________

___________________________________________________________

5. Is she going to work on Saturday?   ________________________

___________________________________________________________

6. Are you going to study tonight?   __________________________

___________________________________________________________

# 24.  Check Your Understanding

**A.  Answer the questions the teacher asks you.**

+ = very good   **O** = good   – = need more practice

1. _________   2. _________   3. _________   4. _________   5. _________

**B.  Make each sentence negative:**

1. Jim is going to play baseball. _______________________________________________________

2. She's going to buy a car. _______________________________________________________

3. We're going to pay cash. _______________________________________________________

4. They're going to see a friend. _______________________________________________________

5. It's going to snow tonight. _______________________________________________________

**C.  Change to a question:**

1. You're going to get a loan. _______________________________________________________

2. He's going to see the doctor. _______________________________________________________

3. They're going to run on Friday. _______________________________________________________

4. The movie is going to end at five. _______________________________________________________

5. We're going to have fun. _______________________________________________________

**D.  Write about something you're going to buy soon** (How much are you going to pay? How are you going to pay for it?):

_______________________________________________________________________________

_______________________________________________________________________________

_______________________________________________________________________________

_______________________________________________________________________________

_______________________________________________________________________________